For Richard
With thanks to friends and family

Published 2010 by CWR, Waverley Abbey House, Waverley Lane, Farnham, Surrey GU9 8EP, UK.
Registered Charity No. 294387. Registered Limited Company No. 1990308.
Visit www.cwr.org.uk/distributors for list of National Distributors.
Scriptures quoted from the International Children's Bible, New Century Version (Anglicised
Edition) copyright © 1991 by Nelson Word Ltd, Milton Keynes, England. Used by permission.
Editing and production by CWR
Printed in China by 1010 Printing Ltd.
ISBN: 978-1-85345-565-0

The Road to
Bethlehem

THIS STORY IS BASED ON LUKE 2:1–20
AND MATTHEW 2:1–12

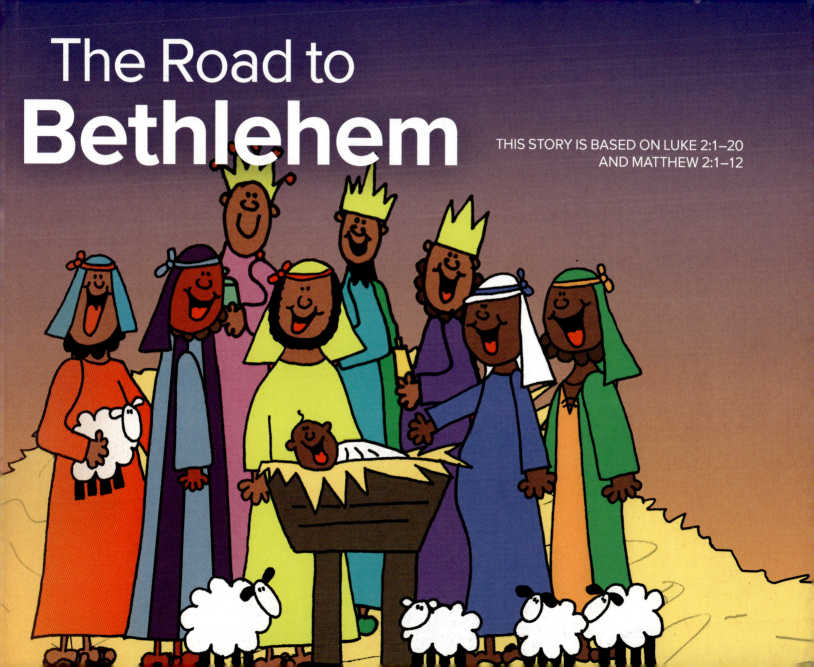

Many years ago,
there was a very rich emperor called
Augustus and he lived in a large palace
at the top of the town.

Emperor Augustus wanted to count
all the people in the Roman Empire.
He decided that he couldn't possibly count
them all on his fingers and toes.

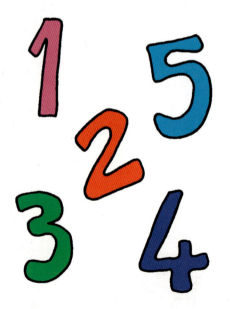

So the emperor thought really hard and ordered everyone in the whole of the Roman Empire to return to the town of their birth. There they would have to sign their names on a big register.

Emperor Augustus was very pleased
with his excellent plan and he went to relax
in his royal bath.

One of the people who had to go to register
was a man called Joseph.
He had to go to Bethlehem,
the town of his birth.
Joseph was a carpenter and made lots of
great things out of wood.

Joseph was engaged to Mary,
and she was going to have a baby very soon.
It was a long way to Bethlehem
where they had to register.
They didn't have a chariot
so they took the donkey.

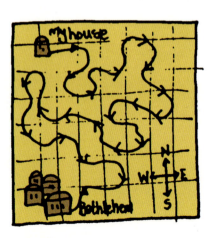

'Ooh, Joseph, it will be
an uncomfortable ride,'
said Mary, as she packed their bags.
She made sure she packed a pencil
to write their names on the register.

Mary and Joseph set off
on the road to Bethlehem.
It was a long, bumpy ride, and Mary was tired
because she was going to have
her baby very soon.
Joseph tried to cheer Mary up. He sang a
few songs and they even played 'I Spy'.

Soon Mary and Joseph were in Bethlehem.
It was very busy –
there were lots of people in town.
Can you see a donkey jam?

Finally, Mary and Joseph
signed the register.
It was very late. They couldn't go
home that night so they had to find
somewhere to stay in Bethlehem.

Joseph set off to look for somewhere to stay. He found an inn and knocked on the door, but it was full of people. He tried another one and knocked, but it was full as well.

Joseph looked at Mary.
She was very tired and she was holding
her tummy. He needed to find
somewhere for her to lie down.
He thought about Emperor Augustus
in his rich palace but he knew they would
never be allowed to stay there!

Joseph tried another inn.
'Please, have you got somewhere we can
stay for the night?' he asked.
The inn keeper said, 'There's no room here.'
'We just need to lie down,' said Joseph.

The inn keeper scratched his beard
and his head and said,
'No but, yeah but, well if you're desperate
I have my stable – that's all I have,'
as he pointed round the corner.

Joseph led Mary to the stable.
It was a lot quieter around there.

Joseph made a bed in the hay for Mary.
He had to clear away a pile of donkey poo!
'Ooh, it's a bit stinky,' said Mary,
'but it will do,' and she lay back on the hay.
Joseph relaxed too and thought
about their journey.

The stars shone brightly in the sky that night
but Mary and Joseph didn't sleep long
because something very special happened.
Mary had a baby!
It was a boy. He was born in the hay.
Joseph had to work very hard
helping Mary give birth.

Joseph wrapped the baby
in strips of white cloth to keep Him warm.
For a bed he used a manger that the cows
had eaten out of!
'Mary, what shall we call Him?'
asked Joseph.

'Can't you remember?' said Mary.
'An angel came to visit me with a special message from God that we were to call Him Jesus – it means Saviour.'

Up on a hill outside town
there were some shepherds dozing
and watching their sheep,
making sure no one came to steal them.

Suddenly, in the sky was an angel!
All the shepherds woke up
and stared open-eyed.
The angel said, 'Hey, don't be afraid,
I've got some great news.
A baby has been born in town and
He's going to be the Saviour of the world –
and you guys need to go and visit Him!'

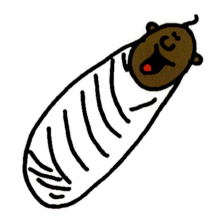

Then suddenly, out of nowhere,
hundreds of angels appeared in the sky!
They were all singing their heads off
in praise to God!

The shepherds couldn't believe it.
They scratched their beards
and looked at one another.
One of them said, 'Eh up, fellers,
we should go and see this baby.
I really wanna see if it's true.
He must be an amazing baby.'
So the shepherds rounded up their sheep
and trundled off into town.

The shepherds arrived at the stable,
tapped on the door and went inside.
Joseph watched as the sheep and
shepherds crowded in.
They told Joseph and Mary
everything they had seen and heard.

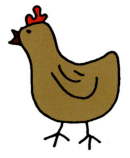

Mary thought a lot about
what the shepherds said.
She knew He would be a very special baby,
but she wasn't quite sure how.

It wasn't until some time later
that three very wise men,
who looked at stars,
spotted a special star in the sky.
They knew this star was pointing out
a very special Saviour.

The three wise men wanted to go and visit the Saviour, so they set off on their camels. On the way, one of the wise men said, 'Excuse me, but how do we know which way to go?' The other wise men said, 'Well, my dear chap, we know because the star is so big and bright. We just jolly well follow it.' So that's exactly what they did.

  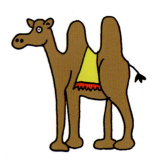

The star guided the wise men
all the way to Jesus.
The wise men bowed down and said,
'We have brought the King
three very special gifts
of gold, frankincense and myrrh.'

As the sun began to rise,
the wise men rode away on their camels.
Mary and Joseph looked at the amazing gifts
and thought about their baby growing up
as a King.

Could a King be born in a stable?
Well, there is much more to tell you
about this story.
You can find out more if you take a peek
in the New Testament of the Bible.
Why don't you take a look?